In Remembrance of a
Special Cat

A Keepsake Memorial

In Remembrance of a
Special Cat

A Collection of
Inspirational Writings

Compiled and Edited by
RICHARD F. X. O'CONNOR

RENAISSANCE BOOKS
Los Angeles

The editor acknowledges with gratitude permission to include the following: "Request From Rainbow Bridge," by Constance Jenkins; excerpts from *The Best Cat Book Ever* by Cleveland Amory, text copyright © 1993 by Cleveland Amory, reprinted with the permission of Little, Brown and Company; excerpt from *All Creatures Great And Small,* by James Herriot, copyright © by James Herriot, Michael Joseph Publishers and copyright © 1972 by James Herriot, reprinted with the permission of St. Martin's Press.

Due diligence has been exercised in attempting to locate all owners of material herein. Permissions have not been obtained from anonymous authors or from those authors not found by publisher despite its due diligence as of the date of publication. The editor would be grateful to receive any updated information.

Special thanks to interns Ryan P. Romines and Michael Mahin who assisted in the collection of the verse in this book.

Printed in Mexico.

98 99 00 01 10 9 8 7 6 5 4 3 2 1

Library of Congress Cataloging-in-Publication Data:

In remembrance of a special cat: a collection of inspirational writings / compiled and edited by Richard F. X. O' Connor.
    p.   cm.
  ISBN 1-58063-004-9 (hc: alk. paper)
  1. Cats—Quotations, maxims, etc. I. O' Connor, Richard F. X.
PN6084.C23117   1998
636.8—dc21
                                 97-44400
                                 CIP

Design by Alex Solis

For Callie
Who taught us of our
infinite capacity to love

&

In loving memory of
Soli, Fred, Gizmo, and Tova Jean

Place
Photo
Here

Inscription

for

(RECIPIENT'S NAME)

In Loving
Remembrance of

(ANIMAL FRIEND'S NAME)

from

(YOUR NAME)

Foreword

From the very earliest days of my ministry as a newly ordained pastor, I was confronted with grief over the loss of loved ones. On such occasions, the Scriptures always held out comfort, hope, and consolation.

Imagine my surprise and challenge when a five-year-old parishioner requested that I conduct the funeral of her beloved parakeet. To this young girl the spiritual well-being of her animal friend was of paramount importance. In recent months I was invited back to that small town to celebrate the fortieth birthday of that young lady and was quite moved to find that the death, grief, and healing of that experience was indelibly fixed in her mind as well as in mine.

Throughout my days of active pastoral ministry, spanning more than thirty-five years, and to the time of my retirement from Norview Baptist Church in Norfolk, Virginia, time after time it was my solemn duty and privilege to offer comfort to those who were grieving the loss of a cat, dog, or other special pet friend. And yes, I conducted other pet funerals invoking divine healing of broken hearts.

Grief is so painfully real, regardless of its origin. The love of, and attachment to, an animal friend can equal that of human relationships. Likewise, the loss of an animal can be just as devastating. May this gift evoke equal understanding, compassion and hope to all in need.

—Reverend Joel L. Morgan
Richmond, Virginia, 1997

Rainbow Bridge

Just this side of heaven is a place called Rainbow Bridge. When an animal dies that has been especially close to someone here, that pet goes to Rainbow Bridge.

There are meadows and hills for all of our special friends so they can run and play together. There is plenty of food, water and sunshine, and our friends are warm and comfortable.

All the animals who had been ill and old are restored to health and vigor; those who were hurt or maimed are made whole and strong again, just as we remember them in our dreams of days and times gone by.

The animals are happy and content, except for one small thing: they miss someone very special to them, who had to be left behind. They run and play together, but the day comes when one suddenly stops and looks into the distance. His bright eyes are intent; his eager body quivers. Suddenly he begins to run from the group, flying over the green grass, his legs carrying him faster and faster.

You have been spotted, and when you and your special friend finally meet, you cling together in joyous reunion, never to be parted again. The happy kisses rain upon your face; your hands again caress the beloved head, and you look once more into the trusting eyes of your pet, so long gone from your life but never absent from your heart.

Then you cross Rainbow Bridge together....

Anonymous
FROM THE INTERNET

Cats pride themselves on their ability to do nothing.

John R. F. Breen

The gingham dog
went "Bow-wow-wow!"
And the calico cat replied "Mee-ow!"
The air was littered, an hour or so,
With bits of gingham and calico.

Eugene Field

I went back and sat down by the bed. Miss Stubbs looked out the window for a few minutes, then turned to me. "You know, Mr. Herriot," she said casually. "It will be my turn next. I have only one fear." Her expression changed with startling suddenness as if a mask had dropped. A kind of terror flickered in her eyes and she quickly grasped my hand.

"It's my dogs and cats, Mr. Herriot. I'm afraid I might never see them when I'm gone and it worries me so. You see, I know I'll be reunited with my parents and my brothers but… "

"Well, why not with your animals?"

"That's just it." She rocked her head on the pillow and for the first time I saw tears on her cheeks. "They say animals have no souls."

"Miss Stubbs, I'm afraid I'm a bit foggy on all this," I said. "But I'm absolutely certain of one thing. Wherever you are going, they are going too."

She stared at me but her face was calm again. "Thank you, Mr. Herriot, I know you are being honest with me. That's what you really believe, isn't it?"

"I do believe it," I said. "With all my heart I believe it."

James Herriot
ALL CREATURES GREAT AND SMALL

W hat's virtue in man
can't be vice in a cat.

Mary Abigail Dodge

"A ll right," said the [Cheshire] Cat;
and this time it vanished quite slowly,
beginning with the end of the tail, and
ending with the grin, which remained
sometime after the rest of it had gone.

Alice in Lewis Carroll's
ALICE'S ADVENTURES IN WONDERLAND

One of the most striking differences between a cat and a lie is that the cat has only nine lives.

Mark Twain

I've got a little cat, and I'm very fond of that.

Joseph Tabrar

Let your boat of life be light, packed with only what you need—a homey home and simple pleasures, one or two friends, worth the name, someone to love and someone to love you, a cat, a dog, and a pipe or two...

Jerome Klapka Jerome

Request from
Rainbow Bridge

Weep not for me though I am gone
Into that gentle night.
Grieve if you will, but not for long
Upon my soul's sweet flight.
I am at peace, my soul's at rest
There is no need for tears.
There is no pain, I suffer not,
The fear now all is gone.
Put now these things out of your thoughts,
In your memory I live on.
Remember not my fight for breath
Remember not the strife
Please do not dwell upon my death,
But celebrate my life.

Constance Jenkins
IN LOVING MEMORY OF ISOLDE JENKINS

Far in the stillness a cat
  Languishes loudly.

William Ernest Henley

If animals could speak, the
dog would be a blundering,
outspoken fellow—but the
cat would have the rare
grace of never saying a
word too much.

Philip Gilbert Hammerton

We should be very careful to get out of experience only the wisdom that is in it—and stop there; lest we be like the cat that sits down on a hot stove lid. She will never sit down on a hot stove lid again—and that is well; but also she will never sit down on a cold one any more.

Mark Twain

A house without a cat, and a well-fed, well-petted and properly revered cat, may be a perfect house, perhaps, but how can it prove its title?

Mark Twain

The Cat. He walked by himself, and all places were alike to him. He went through the wet and wild woods, waving his wild tail, and walking by his wild lone. But he never told anybody.

Rudyard Kipling

Anyone who has had to go through an animal's death knows what it is like to come upon a favorite toy, a favorite ball of yarn, or indeed a favorite anything. Even a dish can do it. But even coming across one of your animal's things is not by all means all of what you must go through. At such a time, even a look at your animal's favorite places will be too much for you, if you are anything like me, you will not only see and hear your animal before you go to sleep—if indeed you can sleep—you will even feel his paws padding on your bed and then, after that, you will dream about him.

Now, of course, there was nothing. No hum, no rub, no pat, no nothing. The whole apartment had, for me, become an empty nothingness. It was not just that Polar Bear was not there—it was the awful, overpowering weight of knowing he was never ever going to be there again.

Cleveland Amory
"THE BEST CAT EVER"

Cats, as a class have never completely got over the snootiness caused by the fact that in Ancient Egypt they were worshipped as gods.

P.G. Wodehouse
THE STORY OF WEBSTER

He seems the incarnation of everything soft and silky and velvety, without a sharp edge in his composition, a dreamer whose philosophy is sleep and let sleep.

Saki

I realize something I did not realize then—how lucky I was compared to so many others who have to face the loss of their animal without other people around them. I, at least, was surrounded by animal people.

And I think they've got to let the person know that it's O.K., that grief for a pet is acceptable, it is normal.

Unlike some people who have experienced the loss of an animal, I did not believe, even for a moment, that I would never get another. I did know full well that there were just too many animals out there in need of homes for me to take what I have always regarded as the self-indulgent road of saying the heartbreak of the loss of an animal was too much ever to want to go through with it again. To me, such an admission brought up the far more powerful admission that all the wonderful times you had with your animal were not worth the unhappiness at the end.

Cleveland Amory
THE BEST CAT EVER

When my cat and I entertain each other with mutual antics, who knows but that I make more sport for her than she makes for me? And who knows but that she pities me for being no wiser than to play with her; and laughs, and censures my folly in making sport for her, when we two play together.

Montaigne

My Love She is a Kitten
And My Heart's a Ball of String.

Henry S. Leigh

Four Feet
in Heaven

Your favorite chair is vacant now
No eager purrs to greet me
No softly padded paws to run
ecstatically to meet me
No coating rubs, no plaintive cry
Will say it's time for feeding
I've put away your bowl
And all the things you won't be needing
But I will miss you, little friend
For I could never measure
the happiness you brought me,
the comfort and the pleasure.
And since God put you here to share
In earthly joy and sorrow
I'm sure there will be a place for you
in Heaven's bright tomorrow…

Alice E. Chase

A kitten is chiefly remarkable for rushing about like mad at nothing whatever and generally stopping before it gets there.

Agnes Repplier

Dogs come when called. Cats take a message and get back to you later.

F. X.

Cat

As if he owned the place, a
cat meanders through my mind,
sleek and proud, yet so discreet
in making known his will that I
hear music when he mews, and
even when he purrs a tender
timbre in the sound compels
my consciousness

Charles Baudelaire

C ats sleep
Anywhere,
Any Table,
Any chair,
Top of piano,
Window-ledge,
In the middle,
On the edge…

Eleanor Farjeon

Last Words to a Dumb Friend

Pet was never mourned as you,
Purrer of the spotless hue,
Plumy tail, and wistful gaze
While you humoured our queer ways,
Or outshrilled your morning call
Up the stairs and through the hall
Foot suspended in its fall
While, expectant, you would stand
Arched, to meet the stroking hand;
Till your way you chose to wend
Yonder, to your tragic end.

Never another pet for me!
Let your place all vacant be;
Better blackness day by day
Than companion torn away.
Better bid his memory fade,
Better blot each mark he made,
Selfishly escape distress
By contrived forgetfulness,
Than preserve his prints to make
Every morn and eve an ache.

Housemate, I can think you still
Bounding to the window-sill,
Over which I vaguely see
Your small mound beneath the tree,
Showing in the autumn shade
That you moulder where you played.

Thomas Hardy

Lovers, scholars—the fervent, the
austere—grow equally fond of cats,
their household pride.
    As sensitive as either to the cold,
as sedentary, though so strong and sleek, your cat,
a friend to learning and to love, seeks out both
silence and the awesome dark...

Hell would have made the cat its courier could it
have controverted feline pride!

Dozing, all cats assume the svelte design
of desert sphinxes sprawled in solitude,
apparently transfixed by endless dreams;
their teeming loins are rich in magic sparks,
and golden specks like infinitesimal sand
glisten in those enigmatic eyes.

Charles Baudelaire

To Winky

Cat,
You are a strange creature.
You sit on your haunches
And yawn,
But when you leap
I can almost hear the whine
Of a released string,
And I look to see its flaccid shaking

In the place whence you sprang.
You carry your tail as a banner,
Slowly it passes my chair,
But when I look for you, you are on the table
Moving easily among the most delicate porcelains.
Your food is a matter of importance
And you are insistent on having
Your wants attended to,
And yet you will eat a bird and its feathers
Apparently without injury.
In the night, I hear you crying,
But if I try to find you

There are only the shadows of rhododendron leaves
Brushing the ground.
When you come in out of the rain,
All wet and with your tail full of burrs,
You fawn upon me in coils and subtleties;
But once you are dry
You leave me with a gesture of inconceivable impudence,
Conveyed by the vanishing quirk of your tail
As you slide through the open door.

Amy Lowell

A cat in
distress,
Nothing more, nor less;
Good folks, I must faithfully tell ye,
As I am a sinner,
It waits for some dinner,
To stuff out its own little belly...

Percy Bysshe Shelley

On the Death of a Cat, a Friend of Mine Aged Ten Years and a Half

Who shall tell the lady's grief
When her cat was past relief?
Who shall number the hot tears
Shed o'er her, belov'd for years?
Who shall say the dark dismay
Which her dying caused that day?

Come ye Muses, one and all,
Come obedient to my call;
Come and mourn with tuneful breath
Each one for a separate death;
And, while you in numbers sigh,
I will sing her elegy.

Of a noble race she came
And Grimalkin was her name.
Young and old full many a mouse
Felt the prowess of her house;
Weak and strong full many a rat
Cowered beneath her crushing pat;
And the birds around the place
Shrank from her too-close embrace.

But one night, reft of her strength,
She lay down and died at length:
Lay a kitten by her side
In whose life the mother died.
Spare her life and lineage,
Guard her kitten's tender age,
And that kitten's name as wide
Shall be known as hers that died.
And whoever passes by
The poor grave where Puss doth lie,
Softly, softly let him tread,
Nor disturb her narrow bed.

Christina Rossetti

And he always spoke of the strange sagacity of that cat with the air of a man who believed in his secret heart that there was something human about it— maybe even supernatural…

Mark Twain

My Cat Jeoffry

For I will consider my Cat Jeoffry.

For he is the servant of the Living God duly and daily serving Him.

For he is of the tribe of Tiger.

For he purrs in thankfulness, when God tells him he's a good Cat.

For he is an instrument for the children to learn benevolence upon.

For every house is incomplete without him and a blessing is lacking in the spirit.

Christopher Smart

My heart, assenting instrument, is masterfully played; no other bow across its strings can draw such music out the way this cat's uncanny voice— seraphic, alien—can reconcile discordant strains into close harmony!…

Charles Baudelaire

It is, of course, totally pointless to call a cat when it is intent on the chase…They are on cat business, totally serious and involved.

John D. MacDonald

She Sights a Bird

She sights a Bird—she chuckles—
She flattens—then she crawls—
She runs without the look of feet—
Her eyes increase to Balls—

Her Jaws stir—twitching—hungry—
Her Teeth can hardly stand—
She leaps, but Robin leaped the first—
Ah, Pussy, of the Sand.

The Hopes so juicy ripening—
You almost bathed your Tongue—
When Bliss disclosed a hundred Toes—
And fled with every one—

Emily Dickinson

Do not stand at my grave and weep,
I am not there, I do not sleep.
I am a thousand winds that blow;
I am the diamond glints on snow.
I am the sunlight on ripened grain;
I am the gentle autumn's rain.
When you awaken in the morning's hush,
I am the sweet uplifting rush
Of quiet birds in circled flight
I am the first star that shines at night.
Do not stand at my grave and cry,
I am not there. I did not die.

Anonymous

One cannot woo a cat after the fashion of the Conqueror. Courtesy, tact, and patience are needed at every step.

Agnes Repplier

In a cat's eye, all things belong to cats.

Anonymous

A Kitten is so flexible that she is almost double; the hind parts are equivalent to another kitten with which the forepart plays.
She does not discover that her tail belongs to her until you tread on it.

Henry David Thoreau

The playful kitten, with its pretty little tigerish gambols, is infinitely more amusing than half the people one is obliged to live with in the world.

Lady Sydney Morgan

Place
Photo
Here

There remains, to those who have lost an animal, two large questions. The first of these involves whether or not to bury your animal. I have always believed that the best place to bury your animal is in your heart. I fully believe that.

The second large question—do animals go to heaven? I do believe that we and our animals will meet again. If we do not, and where we go is supposed to be heaven, it will not be heaven to me and it will not be where I wish to go.

Cleveland Amory
THE BEST CAT EVER

Place
Photo
Here

Place
Photo
Here

Place
Photo
Here

THE FIVE STAGES OF GRIEF

DENIAL

•

BARGAINING

•

ANGER

•

GRIEF

•

RESOLUTION

PET LOSS HELP LINES

Chicago Veterinary
Medical Association/Delta Society
Pet Loss Help Line
(708) 603-3994

University of Florida at Gainesville
Pet Loss Hotline
(904) 338-2032

University of California at Davis
Pet Loss Help Line
(916) 752-4200

The Delta Society
(800) 869-6898